THIS ORACLE CARD JOURNAL

belongs to

_____

THE ORACLE CARD JOURNAL

A Daily Practice for Igniting
Your Insight, Intuition, and Magic

COLETTE BARON-REID

HAY HOUSE, INC.
Carlsbad, California • New York City
London • Sydney • New Delhi

"In a relationship between you and the Mystery, the great God/Goddess, and you and the Divine living planet, there is a sacred relationship where trust is never broken. Only you can break it by forgetting who you are: a spirit in temporary human form."

A Magical Invitation

Dearest one,

If you're here, then you have felt a calling to begin a sacred journey. Perhaps you yearn to find greater meaning in your life, or maybe you ache for a sense of belonging. Perhaps your heart is broken and you need to discover a new way of resilience. Have you stopped trusting your life, gone numb, forgotten your hope? Do you need guidance to reclaim your faith, trust, and hope?

The answers you seek are not within these pages, but this journal will guide you to where they have always been: inside you. The illuminated path to self-discovery is right here, waiting for you to say *yes* to you.

> *You have been chosen . . .*
> *for what you are seeking is also seeking you.*

The stirring inside is an invitation into a profound interactive relationship between you and the Conscious Universe, Spirit, Source, the Divine, Higher Power (or whatever other name you choose) through a most amazing intermediary. Through journaling and oracle cards, you will discover what you're made of, develop your powers of intuition, and explore the myriad ways the Universe engages you, guides you, and illuminates your way forward.

"In the journal I do not just express
myself more openly than I could
to any person: I create myself.
The journal is a vehicle for
my sense of selfhood.
It represents me as emotionally
and spiritually independent. Therefore (alas) it does not simply record
my actual, daily life but rather—
in many cases—offers an
alternative to it."

— Susan Sontag

Why Journal?

Astounding scientific evidence and personal experiences demonstrate that there are many emotional, mental, and spiritual benefits of keeping a journal. According to *Psychology Today*, a journaling practice can "positively impact a variety of outcomes, including happiness, goal attainment, and even some aspects of physical health." And yet so many find it to be a difficult practice to start and maintain!

Have you ever opened a journal and gotten completely stumped about what to write? Did you start by writing "Dear Journal," then sat staring at the page? I remember that feeling well, of wanting to write about something, but you're just drawing a blank. Or your mind is so full that you don't know what to write about first. But when you add the magic of oracle cards, you have a subject to focus on and see where it leads within.

Journaling in this way is not meant to be an intellectual exercise. It's a way to allow your hidden Self to emerge. It's a way to explore your connection to your Higher Power as it comes naturally without effort. It may give you a new perspective from which to view your past and its impact on you, or a way to view your present with greater clarity and mystical awareness. You may find your perception of the world changed, your fears of the present or future removed. Journaling with oracle cards can be life altering.

"To divine is to
imagine the world rightly,
to see past the illusion that
we are separate from the
entire fabric of reality."

— Gwendolyn Womack

The Other Face
Of The Cards:

More than Just Predictions

Oracle cards and other divination methods have long been minimized as "just" tools of the fortune teller, generally expected to be used to see the future and reveal your destiny: "Will he/she/they love me?" "Will I get that job?" And so on. You ask the cards the seductive question "What's going to happen?" to feel in control.

Don't get me wrong: Using oracle cards to see into the future has its place. In fact, I made my living this way for decades. When you ask the Universe what's going to happen, you can get confirmation that you're on the right track, gather information to avoid pitfalls, and view snapshots of probabilities, potentials, and possibilities.

Rarely, however, does the Universe show you things exactly the way you have them in your head. It's so easy to get lost in that Ghostland of the future whose form has not yet been named if you don't have the skill to navigate it and plot a new course. As a professional intuitive and business strategist, I have seen oracle abuse in the form of being so attached to an outcome or potential direction that you give away your power to change.

In this guided journal, you will learn a different and specific way to work with oracles that is not about predictions at all. The daily practice here encourages you to expand your understanding of your Self and remove your masks. It invites you into the awareness of co-creator rather than passive observer. You move from "What's going to happen in my future?" to "What can I do now to shape my future for the highest good?"

"As human beings, our
greatness lies not so much
in being able to remake the
world . . . as in being able
to remake ourselves."

— Michael N. Nagler

Oracles, Me, and Why
I Made This for You!

I 've had a meaningful relationship with oracles and divination of all kinds since I was a child. The first time I experienced divination in the form of cards was through my Scottish nanny, Mrs. Kelly, a spiritualist in her late 70s. She'd take out a deck of standard playing cards during teatime to read for her cohort of curious friends who would visit our house when my parents were out. When she was making predictions, her eyes would look beyond the space we were in, as if into another dimension. When she saw and spoke about something happening in the present or more immediate time frame, the energy in the air felt tangibly different. She'd offer a prediction by tracking events of the future, and I'd sit from my perch on the stairs, entranced by the possibilities. The idea of knowing the future made me feel secure. It was a time I could control, unlike the uncomfortable one I was in.

Mrs. Kelly left once we stopped needing a babysitter, but she still kept in touch. Then, when I was 14, my father taught me the art of tasseomancy. We'd peer into our Turkish coffee cups, reading symbols in the leftover coffee grinds. He also introduced me to the presence of spirit animals, telling me stories from our ancestral Balkan Slavic folklore that centered around animism. This is how I began to understand the profound language of symbolism—the method through which the Universe speaks and the shared language of oracles.

The first divination deck I picked up was the *Universal Waite Tarot Deck*. I was certain the cards could be my gateway into a mystical realm, so I got a bunch of books and learned to use them. I'd love to say I was on a conscious spiritual path ever since, but my late teens and early 20s were a blur. Violence, self-sabotage, and terrible tragedy in my family brought me to my knees, and I hit bottom with drugs and alcohol at the age of 26. I began the 27th year of my life fully on my spiritual path, and have maintained that sobriety one day at a time—for 36 years, in fact, as I write this.

I was two years sober and working as a professional tarot reader while waiting for my big break in music. Then I began seeing a Jungian psychotherapist who just so happened to use the tarot (Haindl) as a tool in her counseling practice. And just like that, a new spiritual and psychological understanding of tarot was revealed to me.

> *Those cards I thought were only for knowing the future, I now experienced firsthand as a way to know myself.*

The therapist suggested I journal with my tarot cards to help me stay on track with what was in my highest good. I will tell you this helped me stay sober and *mostly* kept me out of self-sabotage. The cards always reflected the truth even when I didn't like it or denied it, stubborn as I was— and still am. Mostly the daily practice of journaling and card reading kept me plugged into my Higher Power.

I began my personal journey in earnest in 1986, first learning how to read runes and other divination systems as a tool for self-reflection and self-actualization. Then I found angel cards and Jamie Sams and David Carson's *Medicine Cards*, opening my eyes to the realm of divination cards beyond tarot.

New Year's 1994, I was alone and decided to play around with the idea of making my own oracle cards. I took some playing cards and added sticker labels, numbers, and symbols, then wrote their meanings in a journal. I would refer to my personal deck and guidebook while doing my own daily journal and card-reading practice as well as during my professional tarot readings for others. I was embarrassed to show anyone, but they worked amazingly well. They were my little secret until the Universe *demanded* they be shared!

That scribbled-down system became the foundational structure for my first professional oracle card deck for Hay House. I discovered a new passion: innovating divination systems for the modern seeker. My work became more prescriptive than predictive. I recognized the need for a more empowering, active experience with oracles so that people understood how to influence their future by shifting their present.

It's my life's calling to support you in this way, and I am deeply grateful for this opportunity to share my experience, strength, and hope with you here.

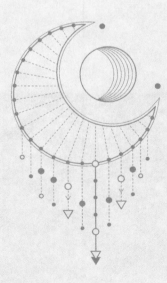

"Know
Thyself."

What You'll Find Here:

Something for Everyone

As you entered the temple of the god Apollo in Delphi, home of one of the most venerated oracles of classical Greek civilization, you would've seen the words on the previous page carved into the stonework. Consider this journal your sacred temple with the same invitation.

You don't need to have any prior knowledge of oracle cards before you begin. In the pages that come, I will teach you all you need to know about what oracle cards are and how they work. You will understand how the Universe works and your relationship to it and learn why oracle cards are the most amazing tool you will want to trust. I'm going to set you up for success!

Once you have the necessary foundational knowledge, you'll move on to the journaling practice. I will give you a framework to follow in which you pull a single oracle card every day, note your impressions, then write about the message you receive with a prompt for self-reflection.

This journal practice will work with any oracle deck of your choosing. You'll find an exercise with guidance for how to choose the right deck, and I include my recommendations for my favorite cards in the back. The most important thing is finding the one that works for you. If you love any oracle deck I have not listed and feel called to choose it, then use that one! This is your journal, your personal journey, your connection to Source. Choose from your heart and you can't go wrong.

If you do the daily practice of pulling an oracle card and journaling, making it a sacred habit, you'll discover that you are never alone, that the Universe is always actively engaged in your life for the highest good, that Truth is always available if you have the courage to ask for it, and that you are a powerful co-creator in a fundamental partnership with the Universe.

Benefits for beginners: By keeping your focus on a daily card, you will naturally get really good at reading the cards in this way. You will discover the layers of meaning in the images and words on the card and in the guidebook. You'll begin to see the universality of human experience and how it's reflected in you. You'll develop an intimate and profound relationship with the deck you've chosen and have evidence that you are always in a meaningful and honest dialogue with the Universe. These same skills transfer to the ability to do readings for other people, if you're so inclined!

Benefits for advanced card readers: You will gain an even deeper understanding of how the cards work specifically for you. You will expand on your expertise as you enter an intimate purposeful experience and understanding of this mystical dynamic relationship between you, the cards, and the Universe. You will see with great clarity that you are always a *story in motion,* never static, always moving and evolving. You'll see your patterns and recognize when you move in circles, and how to move beyond those to choose a new path, a new way better suited to who you dream of becoming. You will naturally move beyond your limiting beliefs and constraints and discover new pathways to follow and explore. Most importantly, you will reveal your most authentic Self—and that has the power to change everything for the better.

No matter how you begin, and from what vantage point or expertise, your intuition will grow and expand. You will just know you are connected to all of Life, seen and unseen, in extraordinary ways. And you will learn to love yourself, forgive yourself and others, and step into the truth of your life's promise and potential.

Are these overly bold promises? Not really. I have worked professionally with oracles of all kinds for over 30 years, and I have used this exact practice for my own self-reflection for even longer. I now also teach it as a foundational practice for students attending Oracle School, an online experiential program I founded for personal transformation that uses oracle cards as our main navigational tool. I have also published 15 oracle card decks and counting (with 3 more in the works) and have a fabulous, friendly Oracle Circle membership community. You could say my entire world revolves around oracle cards!

Trust that everything in here is tried and true. If you're consistent, you will be amazed. No matter what is going on in the outer world, you will see how both the mundane and the magic co-exist, and you will thrive regardless of whatever challenges life throws your way.

> *May you*
> *be blessed with*
> *grace on this journey*
> *of extraordinary discovery.*

Love,

Set Yourself Up for Success

Take up space: There's plenty of room within this journal for you to write and draw, and I encourage you to do so! Whenever I write, I find myself doodling symbols and creating art that enhances my experience. If you feel like you need even more space, there are extra blank pages in the back. You can also purchase a blank journal to continue your journaling practice.

Consider stepping away from the screen: Some people find benefit to journaling electronically. For instance, you can write or create art with apps, record audio entries, and create a searchable system. I am a big fan of handwriting in a journal as opposed to typing, but I will leave it up to you.

Cursive writing on paper takes your eyes away from the glare of the computer, which many of us need a break from. It also slows you down and engages a different part of your cognitive functioning. Studies show that in the raw writing state, you have a tendency to identify more and connect in a deeper way with what you're writing. I've been typing for so many years, and when I switch to handwriting, I am hyperaware of the difference in experience. I feel writing on paper is more intimate, and I'm less inclined to edit myself as I go.

Set aside time to write: Try to be consistent with your practice. Find 10 to 15 minutes in your morning or evening routine that you can dedicate to journaling with oracle cards. For instance, you can write as soon as you awaken, just before sleeping, or before or after meditation or prayer.

Make it special: Do whatever it takes to get you excited every day. If you have an altar, keep your journal, pens, and art supplies there. Light candles or incense, or spray essential oils. Play soothing music. Pray, meditate, or say affirmations before and after journaling. Create your own sacred ritual around journaling.

Take some time now to get comfortable with your journal. Use the following pages to write and draw in a stream of consciousness, without stopping to edit or overthink anything.

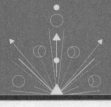

"All the powers in the
universe are already ours.
It is we who have put
our hands before our eyes
and cry that it is dark."

— Swami Vivekananda

Understanding the Universe,

Understanding the Self

E veryone comes to an oracle with their own history, their own idea of what is sacred, their own name for the Divine, etc. Here, I share the terms and concepts that I use. Before you begin, give yourself permission to make this practice your own. Use the terms you are used to, and consider the concepts that make sense to your own worldview.

I use these terms interchangeably, but they all refer to the Conscious loving Universe we are all intrinsically part of and have a unique intimate relationship with:

> *Divine,*
> *Divinity, Source,*
> *The Conscious Universe,*
> *Higher Power, Great Spirit,*
> *the All That Is.*

Next, I refer to the ego as:

> *the small self, or self.*

The immortal energetic soul-self, I call:

> *the Self, or Higher Self.*

We all have an ego; we need it to self-identify. It's not the enemy, as it might appear from the way many teachers speak of it. It's just the vehicle and personality we develop over time through which we experience the world. The healthy ego can serve the highest good while the unhealthy or wounded ego will muck it up. Because it is memory based and self-centered, it is therefore limited.

The Self knows we are immortal, always knows we are connected to Source and made of spirit-stuff, but the small self can't seem to get a handle on that. The energy of the Higher Self is often blocked by our incessant need to see the world through the lens of how we're conditioned. It's no one's fault; it's just how we're made. It takes discipline to stay awake and aware of our connection to the Universe and our capacity to create our futures from the inside out.

Awakening to Your Inner Magic

There's a state of mind I refer to as *spiritual narcolepsy* when we fall into old habits and forget our divinity—and everyone else's too. We lose our spiritual Self and operate from fear and act in accordance with the machinations of our wounded ego. We lose hope and see the world as limited, lacking, and narrow. This leads to polarization and discord.

It's hard to trust a Higher Power, yourself, other people, or even your own dreams when your attention is fixated on what is crumbling around you. We forget there could be a spiritual solution for all our challenges because we're so used to being worried, feeling trapped, complaining, and playing the blame game. Familiarity, even if it's not good for us, is much easier to relate to.

When we see ourselves as fundamentally disconnected, it is an illusion driven by our will, filtered by our memories, and defined by our conditioning. The extraordinary truth is that deep inside you is that greater Self that is always aware of your connection to the Universe. You are a spark of that same vast Divine energy, individuated as a human being. That Self is hidden in plain sight waiting for you to remember who you are.

Did you know you have always had a cosmic blueprint for your destiny within you? To read this map of your life's purpose, you need to awaken your intuitive knowing. You then realize that you are equipped for miracles; you already have all the magic you need. You remember how powerful you are when you consciously partner with the Divine.

The Higher Self is a very effective translator for the Conscious Universe, but it speaks through pictures and images, symbols and metaphors, intuitive hunches, and a deep inner knowing that the logical mind can't comprehend. A practice of journaling and oracle cards helps the Higher Self provide needed assistance to the small self. In working through this journal, you will remember to look within rather than outside for answers. You will rediscover your spiritual connection to the Universe and your ability to participate in cosmic creation—to be the Shaper not just the shaped. You will see all manner of synchronicities begin to rise up in all areas of your life, and the murkiness of life's confusions will lift. As you work with this journal, you'll discover who you really are, what your soul truly longs for, and what you're meant for at this powerful yet chaotic time of transformation.

"To divine a thing is to
discover the intention or
the configuration of the
Sacred in relation to
that matter."

— Dr. Dianne Skafte

Some Background on Oracles and Divination

W ith this journal, you will be using oracle cards to have a direct dialogue with the Divine about your unique personal journey. Since we all have different levels of knowledge and experience when it comes to oracles, I'd like to take the time now to give a quick background on what they are and how they work.

The word *oracle* comes from the Latin *oraculum,* rooted in the word *orare,* which means "to speak" or "to pray." The dictionary defines *oracle* as "Divine message." When we use the word *oracle* today, it can be referring to one or all three of the following forms:

- A person, whom I refer to as an *oracle messenger*
- The message itself, or *oracle message*
- A sacred object or tool used to interpret messages from Spirit interactively, referred to as *oracle tools* or *divination tools*

Divination tools such as oracle cards, tarot cards, runes, astrology, and many other methods have become part of a renaissance of the modernization of the ancient practice of divination. They've gone from being seen as fringe and weird (or completely outlawed) to mainstream (even trendy), as our craving for the sacred has led us outside the rigid boundaries of dogma.

Divination means talking to the Divine, asking for advice, and expecting an answer. This conversation is conducted with special tools through which Spirit may be invited to speak and send messages; the tool we're using here is oracle cards. Divination is a profound way to self-reflect, to get out of your head and into your heart, to nurture that connection between your Higher Self and your small self.

> *And yes, sometimes we can use divination to reach into the future . . . if Spirit will show it to us.*

When we use divination tools, we ask Spirit to reveal itself to us in mirror form. That way we can see ourselves reflected as we exist in the "eternal now," where past, present, and future are all one. In this journal, we will be using our oracle cards to help us remain present, aware, and surrendered to this awe-inspiring partnership.

Oracular Consciousness Is Already Yours

Divination is the act of engaging in a dialogue outside the mechanics and construct of the intellect and five senses, reaching out through *another knowing* to access wisdom beyond the personal self. It's all about moving outside of ordinary awareness to connect with the Divine, a practice that engages another sense, which is (in part) the capacity to access a higher awareness called *oracular consciousness*.

Oracular consciousness is inherent in every being on Earth. It's the pure, observant awareness that's always able to see beyond local reality, that naturally knows how to step outside yourself to touch the strands of truth that often seem so elusive to our grasping minds. This consciousness transcends the confines of time and space and allows us to observe the mechanics of potential and possibility in the past-present-future space-time continuum. It's the part of us that can look at our experience from a nonlocal vantage point. That means our awareness or higher mind can see a bigger picture than our senses and present intellectual mind can measure in a "normal" way.

When you pull your daily oracle card during this journal practice, you are activating a whole other kind of consciousness when you do this with reverence and treat it with respect. The more you do it, the more you'll be open to this expanded awareness. Your intuition strengthens, like you've gone to the intuition gym.

A Modern, Fluid System

Tarot cards, oracle cards, Lenormand cards, the I Ching, the Tibetan Mo, Norse Runes, Celtic Ogham, etc., are all considered oracles, or divination tools. They are all systems of communication that are structured on a language of specific symbols that reflect potential human experience. All of them—except oracle cards—are also considered fixed systems.

A fixed system means that each tool within that system will have a specific, reliable structure. Every tarot deck will always have the exact same number of cards (78) with certain symbols and meanings that won't deviate much from the traditional. The I Ching will always be interpreted through 64 hexagrams. Astrology and numerology are also considered fixed systems of inquiry. The list could go on and on.

The purpose of oracle cards is to enable the same kind of personal inquiry and Divine dialogue as do fixed systems. However, as modern divination tools, they are considered fluid systems because each one is different, based on the creator's choice of structure, theme, and purpose.

I worked with the tarot professionally for years (and still *love* it), but I was longing to create innovative systems inspired by the older ones. This became my passion and the foundation of all my work. Today there are so many amazing, inspiring oracle decks to choose from. You just need to choose the one that feels right to you. It's all subjective, instinctive, and personal.

This journal was specifically designed for you to adopt a sacred practice with oracle cards. However, if you feel called to use another divination system, try it! I believe with a little adjustment, this journal practice can work with almost any oracle.

How to Choose
Your Oracle Deck

So, how do you choose the right oracle deck for you? This will be your companion for your journaling experience. There are many different styles to choose from, with varying numbers of cards and depths of meaning. Some decks are designed to be used for single-card readings while others can be laid out in spreads. Card art ranges from the very simple and decorative to the ornate and rich in symbolism. Some decks have different meanings depending on whether the cards are laid upright or reversed. If there is a guidebook, you will generally find deeper insight into the card meanings, and you might also find meditations, affirmations, or other material. I often prefer to create more complex systems and write substantial guidebooks, but there is no wrong or right way. It's a matter of what you feel serves you.

The way you'll know how the deck is structured is by doing a bit of research. The author will have explained this in their guidebook. You can also find information by reading product pages online, reading reviews, or by watching videos of people using oracle decks. Or, if you can, try them at a store or borrow some from a friend before you get them. You really can't go wrong. I always say the Universe just needs you to pick your tool, then it can go about the business of figuring out a common language between you.

Some people get card decks because they know the author and what they stand for and like their work. If you have a favorite spiritual author, you can see what decks they've written, or which decks they use and recommend themselves. I recommend some of my favorites in the

Resources section in the back of this journal, and you can use the blank pages there for keeping notes on decks and authors you discover.

I think the simplest way of choosing a deck is to sense if you have an attraction to it. But if you need some help analyzing your impressions, consider the following questions:

- Who is the author of the deck? Do you resonate with who they are and what they say they stand for?

- How much experience do they have? (There are some awesome decks created by newcomers in the oracle space, so don't discount any if you're really drawn to them!)

- How does the deck make you feel when you look at the art?

- How does the deck make you feel when you read the messages?

- Do you prefer metaphor and poetry or direct, straightforward styles of writing?

- Does the oracle touch your heart?

- Does it reflect you?

- Does it make you curious?

Trust that you will find your perfect fit; there's no need to get caught in analysis paralysis. No matter what, it takes a bit of time to get used to a new deck, so give your chosen deck a chance to settle in. If after using it for a bit, you're not feeling it, get a different one! You can't go wrong.

"God, grant me the
serenity to accept the
things I cannot change, the
courage to change the things
I can, and the wisdom to
know the difference."

— Reinhold Niebuhr, "Serenity Prayer"

Why Oracle Cards Are the New Self-Care

W hen our heads are spinning and we find ourselves in a reactive, defensive state, we cut ourselves off from Source. Oracle cards can be used as a form of self-care to reconnect us, to plug us back into the current of spiritual power rather than the self-centered desires of the ego. A daily practice with oracle cards, especially coupled with meditation and prayer, is a commitment to a conversation with the Universe. It's a private, personal, and sacred way to stay consciously connected to your Higher Power. It's allowed me to be rigorously honest with myself, to move from my busy mind into the stillness of my heart while staying open to the nuanced ways the mystical intersects with the everyday.

Journaling and Oracle Cards:
The Transformative Power of Living in a 24-Hour Day

I learned the concept of living one day at a time in recovery groups, and it has inspired all my work to date. When I began journaling with oracles, my focus was on staying connected to my Higher Power and living with what arose for me each day. I didn't want to stay stuck in past patterns. Paradoxically, accepting that the only time available to me was the present moment led me to co-create an awesome future!

One day at a time, life unfolded in a most amazing way. I set a course for my dream life, then kept my focus on each moment in front of me. My students have all discovered something very similar: by staying in *today*, a more expanded view of all time frames becomes available in a most uncanny way.

So yes, you can use oracle cards to view the future. But when you do that, remember that you're seeing the *potential* from where you are now. What if there were more? What if you could choose something else?

If you become fixed on a point in time, your focus narrows to how you are shaped by your perceived destiny. *Oh good, the cards said that was going to happen,* you think, as opposed to being curious of what is still possible for you to shape.

> *We need to remember we are active co-creators in our lives—not just passive observers.*

Be the Shaper, Not the Shaped

When you focus on your spiritual connection and hold space for your best life, you become awake to who you could become. Working with oracle cards then helps you stay on track and become aware of your Self, so you can change the patterns in the tapestry of life and move from only being the shap*ed* to becoming the Shap*er*. You are able to meet life on life's terms while forging the path you genuinely desire from the depths of your soul rather than the shallow end of your ego. You transform, and grace comes to bless you unbidden. Even in your darkest moments, you know you are witnessed by the love of the Conscious Universe—even blind, you can have trust in your next step.

I am living proof of that.

A poem read in some recovery groups says: "Anyone can fight the battles of just one day. It's only when we add those two awful eternities—yesterday and tomorrow—that we break down." When relentless and uncertain outer conditions cause you to feel overwhelmed, know that you can get through it one day at a time. When you use oracle cards to reflect on the Source energy that is calling for you to notice it, you turn your gaze inward to the heart and soul rather than outward where you have been conditioned to look for answers. Each small step, dealing with whatever mess you might find, slowly clears the way forward so you don't get blocked by a huge pile of crap you didn't deal with.

That Rearview Mirror Perspective

We think of the past as a place fixed in time, held in place by the stories we assign to it. We create our identities from its muddy soil and thus see through a dirty lens. But the past is fluid. A slight shift in perspective could offer immense clarity.

Engaging in a daily oracle and journaling practice will help you confront those things locked away in the proverbial basement of forgotten, lost, and rejected parts of yourself. It helped me see how my relationship to my mother was limited by my need to be the victim in our story. If I was always in an antagonistic relationship with her, I didn't have to acknowledge my longing and my grief, or even the facts about who she was. But your past shifts when you release your identity as the one wronged. When I moved out of denial, it enabled me to see through a wider, more compassionate lens. I have come to see her in all her extraordinary glory and appreciate the strength she needed to survive World War II and the Holocaust.

Resentments keep us off track and our hearts closed. Today, I experience a very different relationship to the stories that form the lens I see my past through. I am open to love in ways I never thought possible. My old stories have all been rewritten from this new perspective, and it is so liberating.

I pray that your daily oracle card journaling practice gives you the gift of learning to let go and love a little more deeply and surrendered. There is so much more waiting to be discovered.

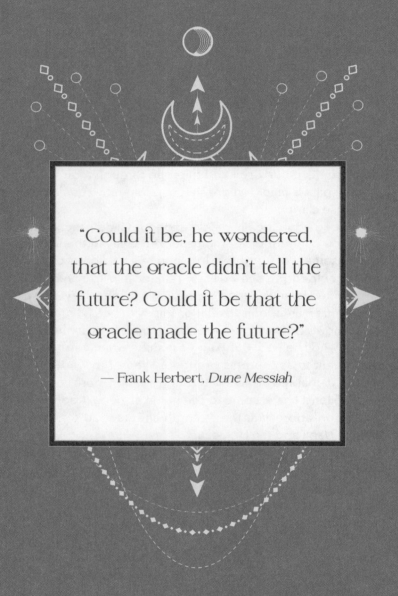

"Could it be, he wondered, that the oracle didn't tell the future? Could it be that the oracle made the future?"

— Frank Herbert, *Dune Messiah*

The Many Magical Functions
of Your Oracle Cards

Oracle cards are an amazing tool for so many reasons. I call them the all-purpose, six-in-one spiritual tool for personal growth. Let's go through them all: flashlight, shovel, magic mirror, communication device, translator, and GPS. I'll also explain how your journal practice will deepen the benefits.

Flashlight

Working with oracle cards is like turning on a flashlight in a dark room. The things in that room were always there, but you might not have seen them without the mystical light cast upon them, which is the insight you receive from your card pull. You then begin to notice the relationship between your thoughts, feelings, and beliefs and the world you experience. You also recognize another type of insight that appears irrational but makes perfect sense—a mystical, more expansive view of what you're looking at.

The light that shines from journaling about the card pull illuminates what is hidden in the shadows too. As we write, we reveal the parts of ourselves and our lives we choose to deny, the parts of ourselves we disown. It's a gentle way to cast a light where we need to bring more love and understanding and compassion for ourselves.

Shovel

No, we're not talking about a real shovel for the garden behind your house, but it *is* a kind of "shovel" for your symbolic Field of Dreams. Oracle cards can help you dig deep into your life, to discover missing treasure, lost parts of your-self, and more. You move beyond the surface of things and get to the core of the matter, where the Truth lies, not the subjective truth of a limited perspective. And you often need this proverbial shovel to move the obstacles in your way, to clear the path you're on so you don't stumble. It also enables you to dig out the spaces for you to plant the beautiful seeds of your highest intentions in your Field of Dreams.

Magic Mirror

Oracle cards reflect the kind of deeper truth you see not with your naked eye but through the eyes of your soul. They act as a magic mirror, showing you the energy and threads of fate that weave through our world from the hidden realms. What you see reflected is deeper and wider and includes who and what is influencing you that you might not be consciously aware of.

Your daily card pull will reflect your dominant energy or the dominant energy in your environment that is impacting you energetically. Sometimes, you may find yourself scratching your head, wondering, *Why is this coming up for me today?* That's where the journaling practice comes in! As you write, the Self comes through so you can see the parallels between what is happening now and how that may connect you to unresolved issues of the past. The card acts as the doorway; writing from the heart lets in the magic of truth and transformation.

Over time, as you fill your journal with your thoughts and stories, a pattern begins to emerge. As you reflect, the journal becomes another sort of magic mirror. You see even more as you gaze into it. You learn to love yourself and your humanity as much as you fall in love with your Higher Power. You experience the truth of both/and: the vastness of your connection to the Universe and to all things, and the vulnerability of all our frail human lives.

Communication Device/Translator

As I've said before, the Conscious Universe doesn't speak English, Spanish, German, or any other language you can think of. It speaks in pictures, symbols, and metaphors, which can be translated through your Higher Self. You experience this conversation not just through working with oracle cards but also the subsequent mental images, intuitive hunches, and nonordinary awareness that begins to flow when we surrender to it. Everything is more than it seems on the surface, and this is what you'll recognize and know as you go.

When I was a few months into my daily journaling practice, I recognized that I was developing an intimate way to communicate with both the Universe and my card deck as its interpreter. It was like the deck and I were learning each other's soul language. At the same time, I felt a profound sense of peace. I felt irrationally witnessed by the Universe and loved by it, fully accepted and cared for through all my flawed and wonderful discoveries. I felt the Universe was figuring out how to talk with me in a way I'd be able to hear it. It's a little like that period when you're getting to know someone who will become a dear friend, or the learning curve when you're figuring out how to use a new device, or both! I have never since doubted that I could have a personal and direct dialogue with the Divine, and I hope the same for you.

GPS

What happens when you feel lost in a world where everyone else feels lost too? Where will you turn? How can you trust your next right action? It's a difficult moment in human history, and we all need tools so we don't lose hope and completely forget our way. Well, oracle cards are the mystical GPS we need.

When you sense you are offtrack but are unclear how you got there or what you need to learn, oracle cards can help you reorient to your True North. When you feel disconnected from Spirit, the oracle cards can help you find your place on the map of your life and discover from which vantage point you're engaging and perceiving your life. You'll know where you are, where you've been, and in which direction you're heading when you regularly work with oracle cards, particularly using the daily practice you'll find here in this journal. And, just like with a GPS, you can set a course: you can set an intention to have a certain experience and be guided there through your oracle journaling practice. I never feel lost anymore, and although I may not like what my cards say sometimes, engaging this practice has kept me heart-centered with steady consistency.

*

What I have witnessed in my own practice and that of all my students is that this relationship between you, your deck, and the Universe is like discovering a hidden door and stepping through it into a mystical land. Then, through this journal practice, magic spills over into all aspects of your life. The whole world starts to show you all manner of synchronicities, reminding you that you're not broken, you don't need to be fixed, you're not alone, you matter, and your life means something. I know you will experience these things too. You just have to commit to doing it.

4 Steps to Prepare for Your Daily Practice

Make a 40-Day Commitment

As with any practice, if you don't actually do it, it won't do what it's supposed to. Journaling sporadically and with a half-hearted, skeptical effort will give you exactly what you put into it. You need consistency to get the full benefit and gifts in here. I've learned that 14 days builds a habit, but 40 days is the perfect number to fully establish your relationship to your deck and develop your partnership with Spirit. Eventually this becomes an automatic habit, and its benefits are wonderful.

Make a commitment to gifting yourself 40 days with this practice. (You can do 40 days straight through, or do 5 days on, 2 days off, for eight weeks.) Set an intention to pull a card a day, then journal about what comes up for you after. This practice of self-discovery invites you to love yourself wholly and completely, to be with your raw self, your flawed self, your needy self, your lustful self, your celebratory self, your fearful self, your joyful self, your hungry self, your heartbroken self, your young self, your rebellious self, your maturing self, etc. All of you gets to be here with you without hiding to discover an essential truth: that you are incredible and amazing and brimming with possibilities and as-of-yet-unseen potential.

Be brave in your vulnerability. You don't have to ever share what's in here with anyone, although over time I guarantee you'll want to share this process with others after they ask, "What's up with you? You seem so grounded and at peace, hmmm, and happy. Did you do something different?" What they're seeing is a beautiful by-product of truly Knowing Thyself. For when you do, you are capable of extraordinary things, and no matter what is happening in the world, your center becomes unshakeable.

STEP 2

Set Your Personal Intention

Now it's time to write a personal intention in a statement that will underline the essence of the energy you're engaging while you work with the cards and journal. It helps to let the Universe know what you're aiming for, although you'll definitely get more than you intended—of that I'm certain.

Reflect on what you hope to gain as a result of working with oracle cards and this journal. What drew you to this book? What whispers in your soul?

Here are some examples of intentions to spark your own creativity:

- To get to know myself better and reactivate my faith in the Universe
- To stay on track with my dreams and authentic desires for my life
- To develop a conscious contact with my Higher Power and see where my life leads me
- To see myself clearly and release my fears as I claim my highest good
- To get to the root of my obstacles so I can be liberated from my past patterns

My intention for working with this journal as a daily practice is

Once you've completed this step, it's time to add the cards.

STEP 3

Activate Your Deck and Mix Your Cards

You'd be surprised at how many people get all worked up about just touching their cards! Obviously if you're an experienced card user, you can skip reading this part. But if you're new, you might be nervous about doing something wrong. So here is a simple way to activate the energy of your cards before you work with them:

- Open the package.
- Take the cards out.
- Look at each one briefly, keeping your intention for this process in mind.
- When you've gone through all the cards, say, "Thank You," over and over. Feel a deep sense of gratitude; gratitude is a simple activator.

Now we mix the cards. Shuffle the cards any way you feel called to. You can do simple overhand shuffles, fancy card-trick shuffles, or lay out all the cards in a big circle on a table and swirl your hands around. Trust that you cannot do this wrong. Trust that your partnership with the Universe is a given. Trust that only good will come of this even if you're uncertain.

Here are a few tips for shuffling:

- For large cards or decks with a lot of cards, it may be easier to handle if you cut the deck into two or four piles to shuffle separately, then combine into a single pile.
- As you shuffle, flip some cards to get a good mix of upright and reversed. (The orientation of the cards can affect the meaning, depending on the deck.)
- Shuffle for at least two minutes, or until you feel like it's enough.

STEP 4

Activate the
Journaling Process

In my own practice, when I decide to start a new journal, I always ask the Universe a question about the process itself: what I need to know about, what it will help me with, and how I might serve the conversation. Posing these types of questions to yourself, then pulling an oracle card to reflect upon it, will help align your practice with the intention you set in Step 2.

These three simple questions will help you get started:

1. "How will this daily practice support me in my self-discovery?"
2. "How will this process deepen my connection with my Higher Power?"
3. "How will this process reveal my innate Potential and Purpose?"

Notice these questions cannot have a yes/no answer. That is because you are in a *conversation*, seeking to understand the subject of your inquiry, not to learn facts about a fixed moment in time. You're asking how deep the proverbial river is, how wide, feeling the flow and the essence of it, and then allowing the magic within you to be revealed.

Before you activate your practice, I'd like to share the cards I pulled as I was creating this journal.

My intention in creating this guided journal has been to help anyone go deeper in their self-discovery through the use of oracle cards and to show the connection we have to a vast ineffable force working in our lives larger than ourselves. I acknowledge that the idea of the Divine often gets tied up by the limitations and implications of language and misunderstood as the territory of religion. By sharing my experience and hope with you, I am asking the oracle to give me the point of this exploration to share with you.

I first asked a variation of Question 1:

"How will this daily practice support a person [you, the reader] in their self-discovery?"

I chose to pull from my own deck *The Enchanted Map Oracle Cards* and received Wide Open, upright, which means:

"You are free to express your uniqueness to the world and share in the bounty of life's endless possibilities."

This line really stood out for me from the guidebook message:

> *This card is the sign of the maverick who freely roams the wide-open space of possibility. Allow for a greater vision to replace old ideas as you dream a grander dream.*

I was so happy because this is precisely the result I hoped for you and the essence of what I've been sharing. We are more than we know, we are more than our memories and conditioning and environments. We are magic and expansive and extraordinary co-creators, and working with this journal will help you realize that.

What comes up for you when you read this? What could your life look like if you moved beyond your perceived limitations? What does your uniqueness mean to you? What else could you make it mean?

What comes up for you as you reflect on this card's meaning? Write about it here and how this relates to your intention.

I then asked a variation of Question 2 for you:

> *"How might this process deepen your connection to a Higher Power?"*

I chose to pull from my own deck *Wisdom of the Oracle Divination Cards* and received Peace, reversed, which means:

> *"Freedom from Attachment, Radical Acceptance."*

In this deck, the reversed position relates to the protection message, which reads in full:

Now is a time for calmness and well-being in spite of temporary conditions. Even if there are dissonant notes in the music of your life, all that means is that you must go within and fine-tune the extraordinary instrument that you are. Find harmony within yourself, and don't look to the outer world to provide certainty. This, too, shall pass, and once again your life will be filled with beautiful music.

This subject is all about letting go, surrendering to life on life's terms, not trying to wrestle or control the outer world but instead turning our gaze inward, trusting the calm within as a way to connect to a Higher Power. Maybe you need to meditate more. What has worked for you? What does it feel like to meditate on peace, on gratitude, and on surrendering your life to the care of that Higher Power? You are an instrument of the Divine. It's so easy to forget that when we get caught up in dramas and harsh judgment, especially in turbulent times.

What comes up for you as you reflect on this card's meaning? Write about it here and how this relates to your intention.

Finally, I asked a variation of Question 3 for you:

> *"How will this process help to reveal a person's innate Potential and Purpose?"*

I chose to pull from my deck co-authored with Alberto Villoldo, *The Shaman's Dream Oracle*, and received Many Masks. I am including the full text here:

We live in a world where everyone we see wears a mask. We wear these masks to cover up and protect who we really are. We learn to do so because we've been conditioned to try to appear a certain way to fit into society. Masks allow us to belong, so we remain within the confines of what is expected.

Masks are not inherently bad. Rather, they provide context and structure for our personalities' and souls' expression. Some of us might believe that a particular mask, fixed and hardened onto us, is our permanent face. We forget that we are living beings, with a multitude of faces, enabling us to experience a fuller, more vibrant world.

Your authentic essence doesn't want to be constrained by others' expectations anymore. Now is the time to strip away the mask you've accepted and discover who you really are. A new self is emerging, and your perception changes as you adopt new ways of being.

Right now it's really important to allow yourself to experiment, to experience the world in all its myriad potentials and possibilities. Try on different masks, and let yourself be fluid and curious. How will you know what you love and what you resonate with if you don't take off the mask you've always worn and test-drive some new ones? Your authentic essence will never change; it will only express itself differently through these optional selves. Through trial and error, you discover more and more about who you want to become. What would it feel like to explore this side of you? Anything is possible if you're willing to open up to your potential. You truly can move beyond the barriers that society has set. Use your imagination and step into the magic.

What comes up for you as you reflect on this card's meaning? Write about it here and how this relates to your intention.

Ready? Now it's your turn.

Don't worry; you cannot do this wrong. However nervous you are, I promise you will get the hang of it.

Shuffle your deck while asking the Universe for clarity on the intention you set in Step 2. Keep any of the three questions in your mind, then pull a card. Once you've written about it, put the card back in the deck, and shuffle again. Repeat the process until you've answered all three.

Remember that these questions will help align the process with your intention and often will reveal other things that will become important as you go.

"How will this daily practice support me in my self-discovery?"

"How will this process deepen my connection with my Higher Power?"

"How will this process help to reveal my innate Potential and Purpose?"

Final Tips for Making the Most of Your Practice

Now that you've had time to process how the deck and journal practice will support you, it's time to *do it*. Asking the right question is crucial. I suggest you begin working with the journal by asking the same fundamental question each day:

> *"What is being revealed for me today for my highest good?"*

Notice that this question is open-ended rather than asking about a specific subject. By asking an open-ended question and writing about the card that reflects it, you will see what message your Higher Power has for you, which may be different than what *you* want to talk about.

This is the way the partnership works. If you trust the Universe, your Self, your soul that always knows better than your ego, then you can enter the exploration with curiosity and an open mind and heart. You stop being the *doer* of your life and move into being the *conduit* for it. The flow state is what this practice fosters.

Understanding the Dominant Energy

When you write in your journal or pull an oracle card with a particular topic in mind, you will often find your desire to focus on one thing being overridden by the Universe. You may not be aware of the energy influencing you at the time of your card pull, but you will quickly see a pattern within your reading or after a few days of journaling.

The pattern will reveal the dominant energy—the message the Universe wants you to know, not what *you* want to know.

Maybe you're impacted by others because you need to set better boundaries. Maybe you're overworked because you've been seduced by the idea you always need to be producing or your value is diminished. Maybe you want to push forward and think it's a brilliant idea, but the card is asking you to pause, rest, and regroup. Be open and willing to move beyond your resistance, your need for certainty, and your fear that you won't get what you want or that you might lose what you have.

No Bypassing Here

Strong feelings can come up during this process, but it's important not to bypass them. Write about them with gusto, and be rigorously honest with yourself even if you're writing about your fears, disappointments about yourself and others, your unmet expectations, etc. This journal practice is your safe haven, and you don't have anyone but you and your Higher Power in the conversation.

Studies show that repressing your emotions is unhealthy and leads to illness of all kinds: in mind, body, and spirit. That said, this is not an invitation to indulge in self-pity or revenge fantasies. It's a way to get honest with yourself about who you are and to move beyond your sorrows to find joy and freedom in your life. The way to get from here to there is not to walk around what you'd rather avoid but to flow through the passage calling for you to heal.

Recognizing the Pattern in Cards That Repeat

In this case, "repeating cards" refers to pulling the exact same card multiple times in a reading or within the space of a few days of your journaling practice. Often it's revealing a pattern in your life and pointing you toward the subject you need more help with. A repeat card might also come up to push you to keep looking, to let you know that there might be more to the card's message, so keep digging! This happened in my own life recently.

A couple months ago, I pulled the card Why from my deck *Wisdom of the Oracle* four times in one week. It turned out that I wasn't clear on my motives—my "why"—when I'd said yes to a project that I was now discovering was not for me. My intentions were good, however, and so when I first pulled this card, I wrote a ton about how great things could be for everyone if it worked out!

The second day I got the Why card again. I knew that I had issues around people pleasing and spinning too many metaphorical plates, so the card made me stop and think. I had to dive into my motives around continuing another project that gave me the same "off" feeling. I knew I had to bow out of the first project, but this one too? Aha! The message was not just about the intention; I needed to write about the potential impact.

Then the third day I got the Why card again. I shuffled for a long time and pulled another card—Why *again*. The Universe was not fooling around! I had to look for what I wasn't considering, dive into the consequences of it all, and understand my why for stopping things. I realized the second project genuinely wasn't in alignment with my values.

A couple days went by, and I was considering the year that had passed and everything that I had experienced. *Again,* I pulled the Why card. I was able to write so much on how, when my motives weren't clear, when I let others decide for me, things tended to go awry. My why is something I must always know, self-investigate, and get genuine clarity on before committing to anything. Had I not done my daily practice, I might have sailed blithely into an overwhelming situation. Thank goodness for my journal and my cards.

What Are You *Making* It Mean?

Ever stop to think that you're assigning a meaning to a situation before actually knowing all the facts? For instance, have you ever had a super-busy friend who gets overwhelmed at work, and you might not hear from them for a while? Do you sit there, hurt, stewing over what a bad friend they are? They don't love you; they haven't called! You refuse to call them because you've decided they abandoned you. This is the track I've allowed my own mind to race down when it comes to a particular friend, and she follows the same pattern with me! So we now make a point of checking in lest our imaginations go wild. We laugh our heads off at how silly we are once we tell the other what we *made* it all mean.

But what about yourself? Have you ever struggled with unworthiness or taking on the emotional baggage of others? Have you ever been in denial about your awesomeness? Have you forgotten to be your own cheerleader? When something is denied you, what do you make it mean? If you get an opportunity but don't feel worthy, even though it's everything you've ever wanted, what do you make that mean?

It's the same concept with the cards and the journaling. What you make the cards mean one day may shift and mean something new later as you dive deeper to uncover your authentic Self. So keep these questions close to your heart as you journal, and allow yourself to be open to possibilities.

*What am I **making** this mean? What **else** could this mean?*

When the Cards Don't Make Sense: The Magic of the Clarity Card

What if you pull a card and no matter how much you want it to make sense, it just doesn't? You have no clue what the heck it's referring to. You want to write about it, but you feel it's not reflecting anything relevant. You drive yourself nutty and get catapulted out of your heart and into your head.

There is always a solution! You will pick a second card: the clarity card.

Pick the clarity card *only* when you truly need more information—not whenever you want to. I need you to pinkie swear right now that you will stick to *one* card a day, and only choose a second card when you are totally stumped.

Promise?

Okay.

By the way, the need to pull a clarity card is not uncommon, and it's also not a sign that anything is wrong. But one thing I should reiterate here is that sometimes a card you pull makes more sense once you've had time to contemplate. If the card's meaning doesn't immediately click for me in the morning, I take a break and write about it before bed. And sometimes I write about my experience from one perspective, but a few days later events transpire that give a whole new spin on everything. The Universe is truly a master of puzzles!

You, the Universe, and the Whole Darn Thing

Life is meant for living every moment with everything it offers you. You're doing this daily practice because you want to know yourself better and listen more closely to your soul and your Higher Power. And you're here to be a deliberate co-creator and step into the mystical river of Life so you can choose your reality and find the magic and meaning in the story of your life, and your purpose for living it. We are living in times that require our bravery and our awareness and our faith in something greater than us. Can I promise you will never suffer and live happily ever after? No. I can say that you will be able to meet everything in your life with grace and develop a greater understanding of the world and your part in it. Willingness is all it takes, and patience too, and kindness, especially to yourself.

Let this journal practice help you reclaim your magic, trust in the Universe, and discover just how amazing and lovable you really are. You have never been broken and you're not broken now. Claim your wholeness and enjoy the ride. Like the late, great Louise Hay always said: *Life loves you.*

I say: *Let it.*

The
40-Day
Process

- Begin with a 5- to 20-minute meditation, and simply imagine you're connecting to your Higher Power. (Go to colettebaronreid.com for a guided meditation you can use.)

- Say *thank you* over and over to yourself.

- Pull one oracle card.

- In the Card Info box representing your card of the day, write the number and name of the card and the deck's name. Feel free to draw in this box, if you desire.

- Fill out the day, location, and other information you want to track on the lines provided, such as astrological dates or cycles you're experiencing.

- Look at the images and words on the card, then write down your first impressions.

- Read the guidebook message, then ask your intuition:

> *"What is being revealed for me today for my highest good?"*

- Write, scribble, draw, and write some more about what the card means to you. Don't edit yourself as you write. Write about whatever comes up—memories, current situations, your feelings—and see where it takes you.

- Every 10 days, take a moment to look back and observe any patterns. There are special journaling pages and prompts provided for you to pause and reflect here.

Ready?
Let's do this.

Card Info

Date:

Location:

First impressions:

Write and draw what the card means to you.

"What is being revealed today for my highest good?"

Card Info

Date:

Location:

First impressions:

Write and draw what the card means to you.

"What is being revealed today for my highest good?"

Card Info

Date:

Location:

First impressions:

Write and draw what the card means to you.

"What is being revealed today for my highest good?"

Card Info

Date:

Location:

First impressions:

Write and draw what the card means to you.

"What is being revealed today for my highest good?"

Card Info

Date:

Location:

First impressions:

Write and draw what the card means to you.

"What is being revealed today for my highest good?"

Card Info

Date:

Location:

First impressions:

Write and draw what the card means to you.

"What is being revealed today for my highest good?"

Card Info

Date:

Location:

First impressions:

Write and draw what the card means to you.

"What is being revealed today for my highest good?"

Card Info

Date:

Location:

First impressions:

Write and draw what the card means to you.

"What is being revealed today for my highest good?"

Card Info

Date:

Location:

First impressions:

Write and draw what the card means to you.

"What is being revealed today for my highest good?"

Card Info

Date:

Location:

First impressions:

Write and draw what the card means to you.

"What is being revealed today for my highest good?"

Day 10: Pause and Reflect

"The Spirit of the world is constantly attempting to communicate with us, but we human beings have forgotten how to listen. So, remember who you are— an intrinsic part of the Great Mystery of life."

Look back at the entries from the past 10 days. Do you see a pattern?

What have you learned so far?

How has your relationship to your Higher Power strengthened?

How have your reactions to life changed?

What synchronicities have you noticed in your life?

Card Info

Date:

Location:

First impressions:

Write and draw what the card means to you.

"What is being revealed today for my highest good?"

Card Info

Date:

Location:

First impressions:

Write and draw what the card means to you.

"What is being revealed today for my highest good?"

Card Info

Date:

Location:

First impressions:

Write and draw what the card means to you.

"What is being revealed today for my highest good?"

Card Info

Date:

Location:

First impressions:

Write and draw what the card means to you.

"What is being revealed today for my highest good?"

Card Info

Date:

Location:

First impressions:

Write and draw what the card means to you.

"What is being revealed today for my highest good?"

Card Info

Date:

Location:

First impressions:

Write and draw what the card means to you.

"What is being revealed today for my highest good?"

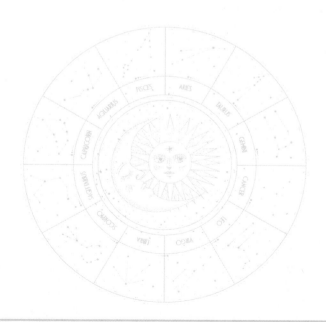

Card Info

Date: _____

Location: _____

_____

_____

_____

First impressions: _____

_____

_____

_____

Write and draw what the card means to you.

_____

_____

_____

_____

_____

_____

_____

_____

> "What is being revealed today for my highest good?"

Card Info

Date:

Location:

First impressions:

Write and draw what the card means to you.

"What is being revealed today for my highest good?"

Card Info

Date:

Location:

First impressions:

Write and draw what the card means to you.

"What is being revealed today for my highest good?"

Card Info

Date:

Location:

First impressions:

Write and draw what the card means to you.

"What is being revealed today for my highest good?"

Day 20: Pause and Reflect

"Anytime you connect to Source and ask for the
Will of the Divine, you enact the Law of Divine Order.
You are able to tap into something that is alive
and loving and infinitely creative."

Look back at the entries from the past 10 days. Do you
see a pattern?

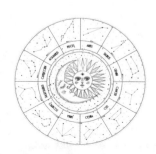

What have you learned so far?

How has your relationship to your Higher Power strengthened?

How have your reactions to life changed?

What synchronicities have you noticed in your life?

Card Info

Date:

Location:

First impressions:

Write and draw what the card means to you.

"What is being revealed today for my highest good?"

Card Info

Date:

Location:

First impressions:

Write and draw what the card means to you.

"What is being revealed today for my highest good?"

Card Info

Date:

Location:

First impressions:

Write and draw what the card means to you.

"What is being revealed today for my highest good?"

Card Info

Date:

Location:

First impressions:

Write and draw what the card means to you.

"What is being revealed today for my highest good?"

Card Info

Date:

Location:

First impressions:

Write and draw what the card means to you.

"What is being revealed today for my highest good?"

Card Info

Date:

Location:

First impressions:

Write and draw what the card means to you.

"What is being revealed today for my highest good?"

Card Info

Date:

Location:

First impressions:

Write and draw what the card means to you.

"What is being revealed today for my highest good?"

Card Info

Date:

Location:

First impressions:

Write and draw what the card means to you.

"What is being revealed today for my highest good?"

Card Info

Date:

Location:

First impressions:

Write and draw what the card means to you.

"What is being revealed today for my highest good?"

Card Info

Date:

Location:

First impressions:

Write and draw what the card means to you.

"What is being revealed today for my highest good?"

Day 30: Pause and Reflect

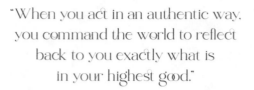

"When you act in an authentic way,
you command the world to reflect
back to you exactly what is
in your highest good."

Look back at the entries from the past 10 days. Do you see a pattern?

What have you learned so far?

How has your relationship to your Higher Power strengthened?

How have your reactions to life changed?

What synchronicities have you noticed in your life?

Card Info

Date:

Location:

First impressions:

Write and draw what the card means to you.

"What is being revealed today for my highest good?"

Card Info

Date:

Location:

First impressions:

Write and draw what the card means to you.

"What is being revealed today for my highest good?"

Card Info

Date:

Location:

First impressions:

Write and draw what the card means to you.

"What is being revealed today for my highest good?"

Card Info

Date:

Location:

First impressions:

Write and draw what the card means to you.

"What is being revealed today for my highest good?"

Card Info

Date:

Location:

First impressions:

Write and draw what the card means to you.

"What is being revealed today for my highest good?"

Card Info

Date:

Location:

First impressions:

Write and draw what the card means to you.

"What is being revealed today for my highest good?"

Card Info

Date:

Location:

First impressions:

Write and draw what the card means to you.

"What is being revealed today for my highest good?"

Card Info

Date:

Location:

First impressions:

Write and draw what the card means to you.

"What is being revealed today for my highest good?"

Card Info

Date:

Location:

First impressions:

Write and draw what the card means to you.

Card Info

Date:

Location:

First impressions:

Write and draw what the card means to you.

"What is being revealed today for my highest good?"

Day 40: Pause and Reflect

"Always remember that you have the capacity and responsibility to shape reality in the best way possible regardless of what challenges life brings."

Look back at the entries from the past 10 days. Do you see a pattern?

What have you learned so far?

How has your relationship to your Higher Power strengthened?

How have your reactions to life changed?

What synchronicities have you noticed in your life?

40 Days of Reflection

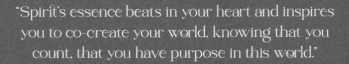

"Spirit's essence beats in your heart and inspires you to co-create your world, knowing that you count, that you have purpose in this world."

You've done it! You've completed 40 days of this journaling with oracle cards practice. Now look back at *all* your entries over the past weeks. Do you see a pattern?

- Look back at the intention you set when you started this journal. Do you feel it has been fulfilled? What new intention can you set for yourself now?

- How did this practice support you in your self-discovery? What did you learn about yourself? The Divine? The Universe?

- What is the state of your relationship with your Higher Power?

- How have your reactions to life changed? How has your *life* changed?

- Where in your life have you been an active co-creator and not just an observer?

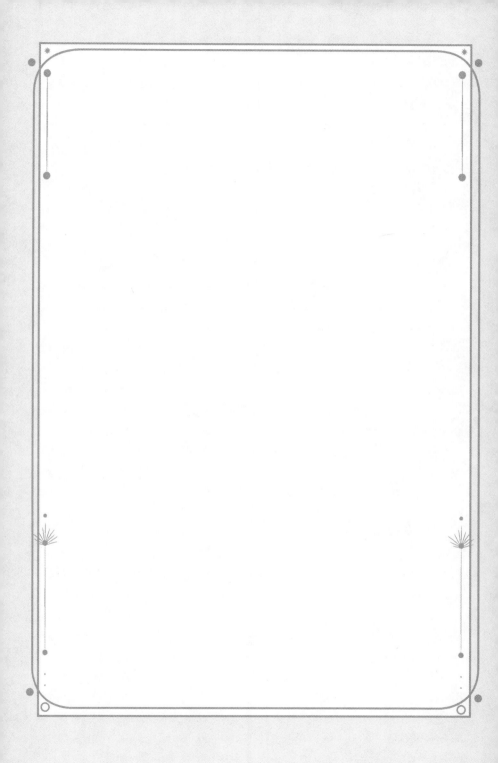

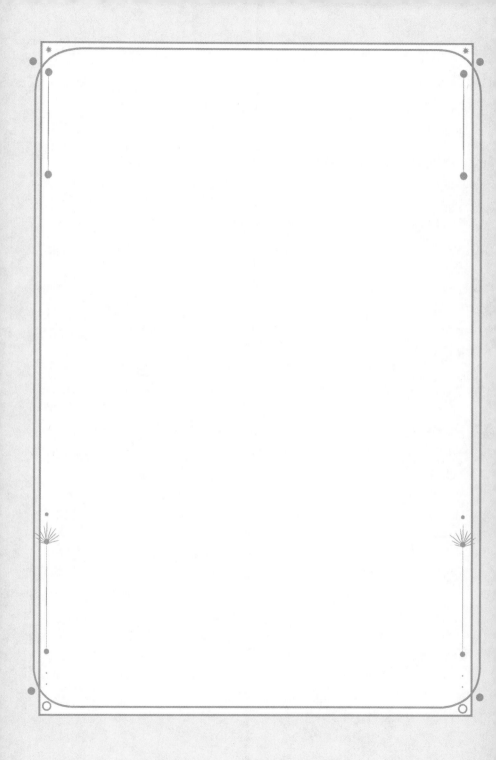

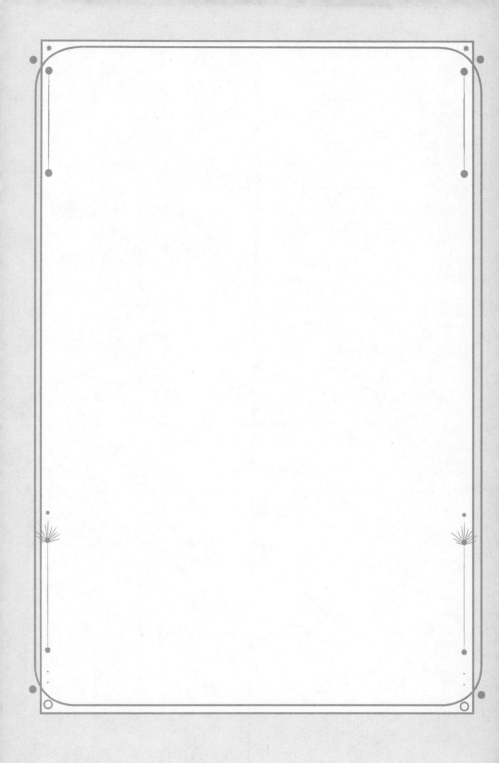

Resources

RECOMMENDED DECKS

These are the decks I have personally used and liked for this process:

Mine: *Wisdom of the Oracle Divination Cards*,
The Shaman's Dream Oracle (with Alberto Villoldo, Ph.D.),
The Enchanted Map Oracle Cards, *Crystal Spirits Oracle*,
The Spirit Animal Oracle

Abiola Abrams: *African Goddess Rising Oracle*

Alana Fairchild: *Sacred Rebels Oracle*, *Mother Mary Oracle*

Angelina Mirabito, Ph.D.: *The Lantern Oracle*

Chris-Anne: *The Sacred Creators Oracle*

Denise Linn: *Sacred Destiny Oracle*,
Sacred Traveler Oracle Cards

Jamie Sams & David Carson: *Medicine Cards*

Juliet Diaz & Lorriane Anderson: *The Earthcraft Oracle*

Justin Moikeha Asar: *Liquid Crystal Oracle*

Krystal Banner: *The Price of Love Oracle*

Kyle Gray: *Angels and Ancestors Oracle Cards*

Radleigh Valentine: *The Archangel Michael
Sword of Light Oracle*

Rebecca Campbell: *The Starseed Oracle*

Sandra Anne Taylor: *Energy Oracle Cards*

Shaheen Miro: *The Lunar Nomad Oracle*

ORACLE SCHOOL®

Deepen your experience of the process you just undertook with Oracle School, the first online training of its kind. Continue exploring your connection with oracle cards, the Universe, and yourself. Tap into your natural intuitive gifts and the infinite wisdom of the Universe. And make empowered choices to manifest a life you love. Enrollment opens annually, so get on the waitlist now. www.colettebaronreid.com/oracle-school-waitlist

ORACLE CIRCLE MEMBERSHIP

The Oracle Circle is a safe, courageous, and authentic community where you'll explore how astrology, oracle cards, numerology and energetic cycles play a role in your life's path. Think of it as going to the spiritual gym! You'll receive a plethora of mystical gifts, live monthly community calls with Colette, exclusive readings and spreads, and more.

So if you want to feel at peace within a friendly, supportive community and be confident that you have all the spiritual tools you need to face whatever comes your way, the Oracle Circle is calling out to you. www.cbrlove.com

ORACLE CARD READER COURSES

The Magic of Journaling with Oracle Cards: Continue deepening your experience with this journal along with me in this course. www.hayhouseu.com

Oracle Cards 101: In just 5 minutes a day, you can learn to read the oracle cards with confidence, so you never miss another Divine message! www.colettebaronreid.com

The Certified Card Reader Course: Master the mystical art of card reading and—if you so choose—create a fulfilling spiritual business, guided by multiple world-renowned teachers (including me!) in this premiere online course. www.hayhouseu.com

Also by Colette Baron-Reid

Books

The Map

Messages from Spirit

Remembering the Future

Uncharted

Card Decks

Mystical Shaman Oracle Cards
(with Alberto Villoldo and Marcela Lobos)

The Shaman's Dream Oracle (with Alberto Villoldo)

The Crystal Spirits Oracle

The Enchanted Map Oracle Cards

Goddess Power Oracle

The Good Tarot

The Oracle of E (with Pam Grout)

Oracle of the 7 Energies

Postcards from Spirit

The Spirit Animal Oracle

The Wisdom of Avalon Oracle Cards

Wisdom of the Hidden Realms Oracle Cards

Wisdom of the Oracle Divination Cards

All of the above are available at your local bookstore, or may be ordered by visiting:

Hay House USA: www.hayhouse.com®
Hay House Australia: www.hayhouse.com.au
Hay House UK: www.hayhouse.co.uk
Hay House India: www.hayhouse.co.in

About the Author

Colette Baron-Reid is an internationally respected spiritual intuitive, psychic medium, educator, and oracle expert. Her best-selling books and oracle cards are published worldwide in 27 languages. She is the founder of Oracle School, a global online learning platform with students in 26 countries, where self-empowerment, co-creation, and ancient oracles meet in a modern, contemporary way. She is the host of *Inside the Wooniverse*, a weekly podcast series featuring authentic and playful conversations with some of the world's most interesting sages, scientists, and celebrities. Colette is also the creator of the energy psychology technique the Invision Process®. She spends her time between Canada and the U.S. with her husband and two Pomeranians.

Colette is the author of *Remembering the Future*; *Messages from Spirit*; *The Map*; *Uncharted*; and the best-selling oracle decks *The Wisdom of Avalon Oracle Cards*, *Wisdom of the Hidden Realms Oracle Cards*, *The Enchanted Map Oracle Cards*, *Wisdom of the Oracle Divination Cards*, *Postcards from Spirit*, and more.

Website: colettebaronreid.com

We hope you enjoyed this Hay House book. If you'd like to receive our online catalog featuring additional information on Hay House books and products, or if you'd like to find out more about the Hay Foundation, please contact:

Hay House, Inc., P.O. Box 5100, Carlsbad, CA 92018-5100
(760) 431-7695 or (800) 654-5126
(760) 431-6948 (fax) or (800) 650-5115 (fax)
www.hayhouse.com® • www.hayfoundation.org

————

Published in Australia by: Hay House Australia Pty. Ltd.,
18/36 Ralph St., Alexandria NSW 2015
Phone: 612-9669-4299 • *Fax:* 612-9669-4144
www.hayhouse.com.au

Published in the United Kingdom by: Hay House UK, Ltd.,
The Sixth Floor, Watson House, 54 Baker Street, London W1U 7BU
Phone: +44 (0)20 3927 7290 • *Fax:* +44 (0)20 3927 7291
www.hayhouse.co.uk

Published in India by: Hay House Publishers India,
Muskaan Complex, Plot No. 3, B-2, Vasant Kunj, New Delhi 110 070
Phone: 91-11-4176-1620 • *Fax:* 91-11-4176-1630
www.hayhouse.co.in

————

Access New Knowledge.
Anytime. Anywhere.

Learn and evolve at your own pace
with the world's leading experts.

www.hayhouseU.com